Find Santa Claus as He Brings Christmas Joy

Cover illustrated by Paul Sharp
Illustrated by Jerry Tiritilli

Louis Weber, C.E.O.
Publications International, Ltd.
7373 North Cicero Avenue
Lincolnwood, Illinois 60712

www.pubint.com

Manufactured in China.

8 7 6 5 4 3 2 1

ISBN 0-7853-3940-X

PUBLICATIONS INTERNATIONAL, LTD.

Everyone loves to decorate for Christmas! And of course, "yours truly" appears in many wonderful decorations. Check out this craft show—I'm a hot item this year! See if you can find me in all these crafts. Don't forget to find the real me, too!

2 Santa cookies

A Santa stocking

A wooden Santa doll

A Santa wreath

A Santa lamp

A Santa quilt

A Santa pillow

Santa in a centerpiece

RIVER CITY HIGH SCHOOL
CRAFT SHOW
CKETS
CRAFT SALE TODAY
SCHOOL GYM
GARLAND
GARLIC
PORTRAITS
TREE SKIRTS
PILLOWS
HAIR BOWS
WATERCOLOR#9

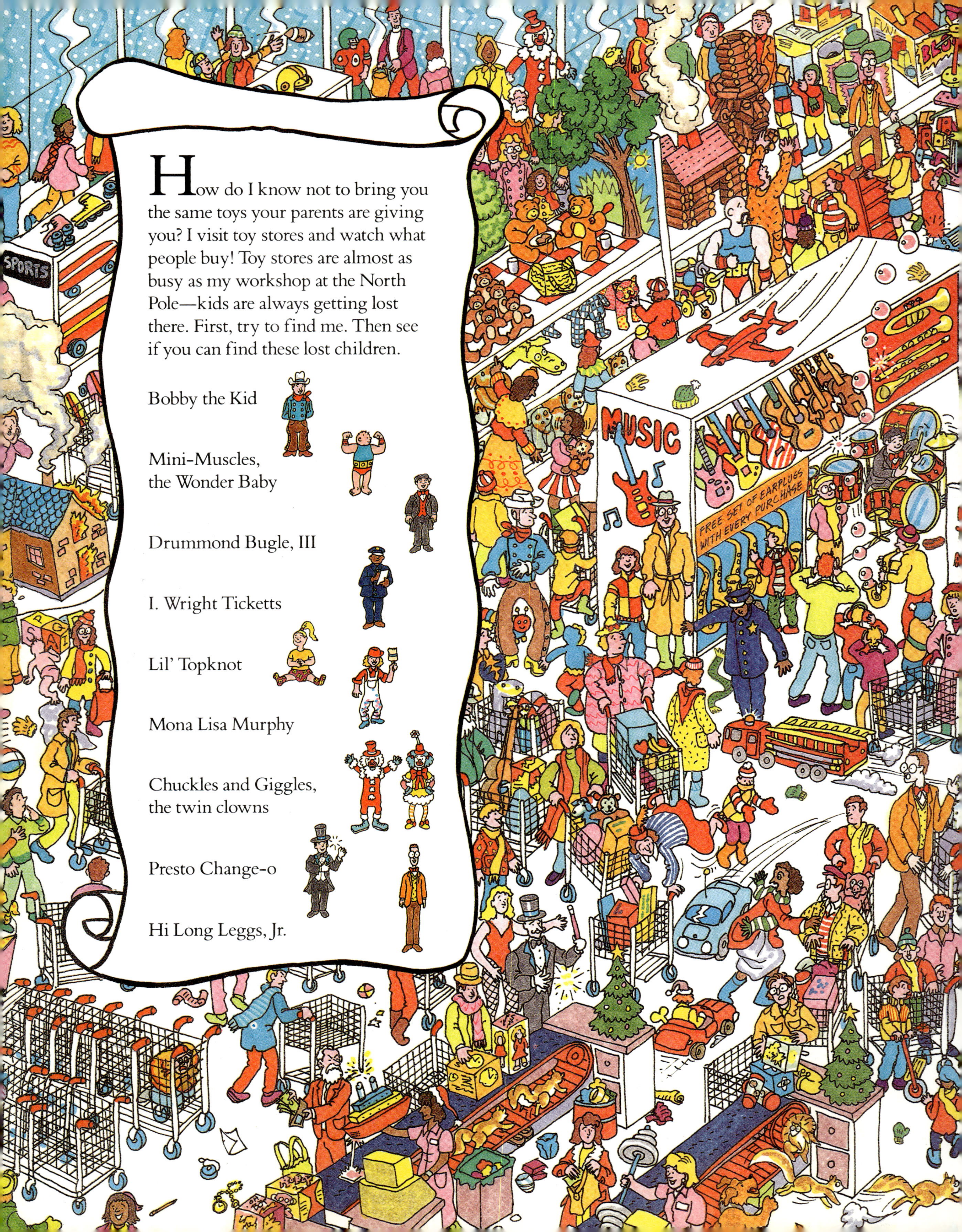

How do I know not to bring you the same toys your parents are giving you? I visit toy stores and watch what people buy! Toy stores are almost as busy as my workshop at the North Pole—kids are always getting lost there. First, try to find me. Then see if you can find these lost children.

Bobby the Kid

Mini-Muscles, the Wonder Baby

Drummond Bugle, III

I. Wright Ticketts

Lil' Topknot

Mona Lisa Murphy

Chuckles and Giggles, the twin clowns

Presto Change-o

Hi Long Leggs, Jr.

CRAFTY CORNER
CLAY
DOLLS
SALE
TANTRUM TIMMY
BABY UPCHUCK
MS TALK A LOT
BETTY WETTY
TRACE TEARS
FINISH LINE
PLAY KITCHEN TOYS
PLASTIC FOOD
CROQUET SET

One of my favorite things about Christmas is that I get to visit with girls and boys who come to see me at shopping malls. Shopping malls can be pretty crazy at Christmas, though! I'm taking a break right now. Can you find me? Can you find these crazy Christmas shoppers, too?

- Tarzan
- Candi Cotton
- Moe Hawk
- Kringles the Klown
- Curly Wiggs
- Leif Eric's son
- Mother Goose
- M. T. Pocketts

HOUSE CONSTRUCTION
JOE'S PET STORE
CLOSED BE BACK
JEWELRY
PIZZA
WE DELIVER
HATS
WE R SHOES
WE R SHOES
99% OFF SALE
GOLF BALLS
NAUGHTY CHILDREN
KICK ME
368 SHOPPING DAYS UNTIL NEXT CHRISTMAS
SANTA IS FEEDING HIS REINDEER
WILL RETURN
NICE CHILDREN

Christmas is only a few days away. And if you think it is busy at your house, you should see my workshop! Do you think I'll be ready for my Christmas Eve ride? After you find me, help me find these toys to fill my sack. We'd better check the list twice!

A red wagon

A train

A doll

A tricycle

A teddy bear

A ball

A skateboard

A truck

MERRY CHRISTMAS

'Twas the night before Christmas,
and all through these houses,
People were still up,
Including some mouses!

Well, this isn't *exactly* the way my favorite poem goes, but my way is more realistic! See if you can find me, and then see if you can spot these Christmas Eve classics.

Cookies and milk left out for me

A mouse not stirring

This stocking hung by the chimney with care

2 fathers in sleeping caps

Sugarplums dancing

4 children nestled all snug in their beds

SANTA
SANTA

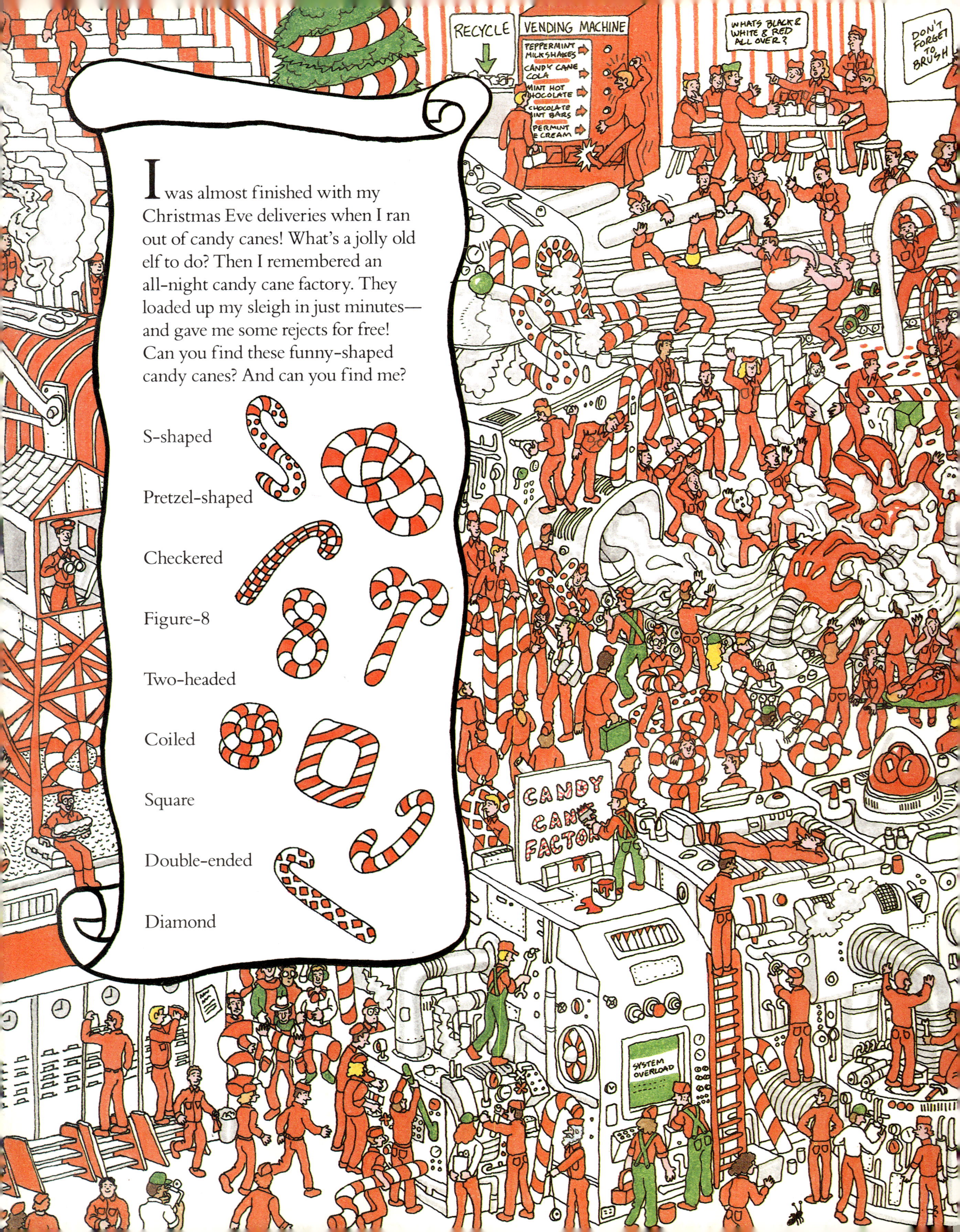

I was almost finished with my Christmas Eve deliveries when I ran out of candy canes! What's a jolly old elf to do? Then I remembered an all-night candy cane factory. They loaded up my sleigh in just minutes—and gave me some rejects for free! Can you find these funny-shaped candy canes? And can you find me?

S-shaped

Pretzel-shaped

Checkered

Figure-8

Two-headed

Coiled

Square

Double-ended

Diamond

NEW DENTAL PLAN
SEE PERSON
REJECTS
CANDY CANE RAPPER
SUGAR
PLAY

Most people think I only fly through the air to deliver Christmas gifts. The mermaids, mermen, and other sea creatures will tell you differently. In fact, I swim so well, they think I'm one of them! Can you find me? Can you find this other silly sea stuff?

A Christmas seal

All eight of my reindeer

An angelfish

A catfish

5 notes in bottles

A peanut-butter-and-jellyfish

A submarine

A hammerhead shark

BUOYS
GULLS
S.S. MINNOW
CANDY CANE CLIPPER
S.S. RUDOLPH
SPIRIT OF CHRISTMAS
GOOD SHIP LOLLIPOP
CHRISTMAS SEAL
CAROLS
PEACE!

I had "wrapped up" my Christmas Eve rounds, when I realized I hadn't wrapped my gift to Mrs. Claus yet! I stopped off at Worldwide Gift Wrap, Inc. to see if they could help me out. Boy, were they busy! I decided to wrap Mrs. Claus's fuzzy slippers myself. After you find me, see if you can find these things that will help me wrap my gift.

A pair of yellow scissors

A red ruler

A stapler

Candy-cane wrapping paper

A pencil

A green tape dispenser

A snowman card

A green shoebox

WORLDWIDE GIFT WRAP, INC.
We've got it covered!
GIFT WRAP WHILE-U-WAIT
WRAP & SHIP
SNACKS
PROFITS
GIFT WRAP WHILE-U-WAIT
SNACK BAR
BOSS' OFFICE
BOX DEPARTMENT
PAPER PRINTING PRESSES
BOX OFFICE
TISSUES
TOP SECRET! KEEP A LID ON IT!
BOX SEAT

Mrs. Santa thinks I've put on a little weight lately. She suggested I take up skiing and skating. The ski lessons were fun, but it went downhill after that! After you find me, see if you can find these other silly skiers and skaters.

A real rockin' skier

A skier in a fur coat

A real cool dude

Somebody who's all "wrapped up" in skiing

"Duck!"

A skier who's "out of this world!"

A "figure" skater

Wroger Wrongway

HO
HO
HO
EAD MAN'S
DROP
RIP
BONEBREAK HOTEL
BUNNY
SLOPE
DANGER
MEN AT WORK

Take another look at the houses in *The Night Before Christmas* scene. Can you find these other funny things?

- ☐ Grandma got run over by a reindeer
- ☐ A Frantic Dad
- ☐ A Sudsy "Santa"
- ☐ A "cool" dog house
- ☐ A cat burglar
- ☐ A snowman who's out of this world

Grab your wallet and head back into to *Craft Show!* Can you find these silly things?

- ☐ A runaway gingerbread man
- ☐ A "door" prize
- ☐ A pickpocket plant
- ☐ Paul Bunyan's mom
- ☐ A pig in a blanket
- ☐ Pinocchio
- ☐ A *real fruit* cake
- ☐ A vampire

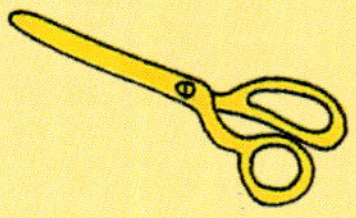

Dive back into the *Ocean* scene, and see if you can find these other funny things:

- ☐ A seahorse race
- ☐ An oyster bed
- ☐ A "cave" with an appetite
- ☐ The Good Ship Lollipop
- ☐ Three men in a tub
- ☐ A hotdog surfer
- ☐ A gold miner
- ☐ A school of fish

Hope you've got a sweet tooth! Go back to the *Candy Cane Factory* and look for these things:

- ☐ A sweet snowman
- ☐ A candy cane rapper
- ☐ A candy cane napper
- ☐ A guy with ants in his pants
- ☐ A worker carried away by his job
- ☐ A worker whose bubble hasn't burst

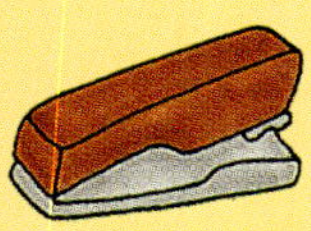